120 GREAT
MARITIME PAINTINGS

CD-ROM & BOOK

Edited by
Carol Belanger Grafton

DOVER PUBLICATIONS, INC.
Mineola, New York

Planet Friendly Publishing
✓ Made in the United States
✓ Printed on Recycled Paper
 Text: 10% Cover: 10%
Learn more: www.greenedition.org

At Dover Publications we're committed to producing books in an earth-friendly manner and to helping our customers make greener choices.

Manufacturing books in the United States ensures compliance with strict environmental laws and eliminates the need for international freight shipping, a major contributor to global air pollution.

And printing on recycled paper helps minimize our consumption of trees, water and fossil fuels. The text of *120 Great Maritime Paintings CD-ROM & Book* was printed on paper made with 10% post-consumer waste, and the cover was printed on paper made with 10% post-consumer waste. According to Environmental Defense's Paper Calculator, by using this innovative paper instead of conventional papers, we achieved the following environmental benefits:

Trees Saved: 6 • Air Emissions Eliminated: 487 pounds
Water Saved: 2,342 gallons • Solid Waste Eliminated: 142 pounds

For more information on our environmental practices, please visit us online at www.doverpublications.com/green

---

The CD-ROM inside this book contains all of the images. There is no installation necessary. Just insert the CD into your computer and call the images into your favorite software (refer to the documentation with your software for further instructions). Each image has been scanned at 300 dpi and saved in both 72-dpi Internet-ready and 300-dpi high-resolution JPEG format.

The "Images" folder on the CD contains two different folders. All of the high resolution JPEG files have been place in one folder and all of the Internet-ready JPEG files can be found in the other folder. The images in each of these folders are identical. Every image has a unique file name in the following format: xxx.xxx. The first 3 digits of the file name, before the period, correspond to the number printed with the image in the book. The last 3 letters of the file name "JPEG," refer to the file format. So, 001.JPEG would be the first file in the JPEG folder.

Also included on the CD-ROM is Dover Design Manager, a simple graphics editing program for Windows that will allow you to view, print, crop, and rotate the images.

For technical support, contact:
 Telephone: 1 (617) 249-0245
 Fax: 1 (617) 249-0245
 Email: dover@artimaging.com
 Internet: **http://www.dovertechsupport.com**
The fastest way to receive technical support is via email or the Internet.

Bibliographical Note

120 Great Maritme Paintings CD-ROM & Book, edited by Carol Belanger Grafton, is a new work, first published by Dover Publications, Inc., in 2009.

Dover Electronic Clip Art®

International Standard Book Number
ISBN-13: 978-0-486-99037-8
ISBN-10: 0-486-99037-0

Manufactured in the United States by Courier Corporation
99037001
www.doverpublications.com

001. LUDOLF BACKHUYSEN
A Wijdschip, a Smalschip and a States Yacht Tacking; n.d.

002. LUDOLF BACKHUYSEN
Dutch Vessels on a Stormy Sea; c. 1690

003. GEORGE BELLOWS
The Big Dory; 1913

004. THOMAS BIRCH
The Macedonian *and the* United States; 1812

005. THOMAS BIRCH
The Battery and Harbor; 1811

006. JOHN BLUNT
Boston Harbor; 1835

007. EUGENE BOUDIN
Quay at Honfleur; 1865

008. EUGENE BOUDIN
Etretat, the Porte d'Aval; 1890

009. EUGENE BOUDIN
Quay at Villefranche; 1892

010. EUGENE BOUDIN
Beach at Trouville; 1863

011. WILLIAM BRADFORD
Ships in Boston Harbor at Twilight; 1859

012. JULES BRETON
A Spring by the Sea; 1866

014. JAMES E. BUTTERSWORTH
The Schooner Mohawk *off Sandy Hook Lighthouse;* n.d.

015. JAMES E. BUTTERSWORTH
Yachts Rounding the Mark; c. 1875

016. JAMES E. BUTTERSWORTH
Columbia *leading* Dauntless *in the Hurricane Cup Race*; n.d.

017. GUSTAVE CAILLEBOTTE
Regatta at Villerville; 1884

018. JAN VAN DE CAPPELLE
Shipping in a Calm at Flushing with a States General Yacht Firing a Salute; 1649

019. JAN VAN DE CAPPELLE
Shipping in Calm Waters of an Estuary, a Harbor Town in the Distance; 1650

020. MARY CASSATT
Children at the Seashore; 1885

021. LORENZO CASTRO
The Battle of Actium, 2 September 31 BC; 1672

022. WILLIAM MERRITT CHASE
At the Seaside; 1892

023. NICHOLAS MATTHEW CONDY
Mr. Ward and his Family on Board his Cutter Guerrilla; c. 1840

024. JOHN SELL COTMAN
Fishing Boats off Yarmouth; n.d.

025. GUSTAVE COURBET
The Porte d'Aval at Etretat; 1869

026. GUSTAVE COURBET
The Fishing Boat; 1865

027. GUSTAVE COURBET
The Shore at Trouville: Sunset Effect; c. 1865/69

028. FREDERIC SCHILLER COZZENS
Off Brenton's Reef; 1883

029. NATHANIEL CURRIER and JAMES MERRITT IVES
The Yacht Squadron at Newport; 1872

030. AELBERT CUYP
The Maas at Dordrecht; c. 1650

031. EUGENE DELACROIX
Shipwreck on the Coast; 1862

032. THOMAS EAKINS
Starting Out after Rail; 1874

033. FLEMISH SCHOOL
The Wreck of the Amsterdam; c. 1610s

034. CASPAR DAVID FRIEDRICH
Moonrise at the Sea; 1822

035. CASPAR DAVID FRIEDRICH
The Sea of Ice; 1823-24

036. CASPAR DAVID FRIEDRICH
Periods of Life; 1834-35

037. THOMAS GAINSBOROUGH
A Rocky Coastal Scene; 1781

038. PAUL GAUGUIN
Bathers at Dieppe; 1885

039. PAUL GAUGUIN
Seascape; 1886

040. VINCENT VAN GOGH
Boats on the Beach at Saintes-Maries; 1888

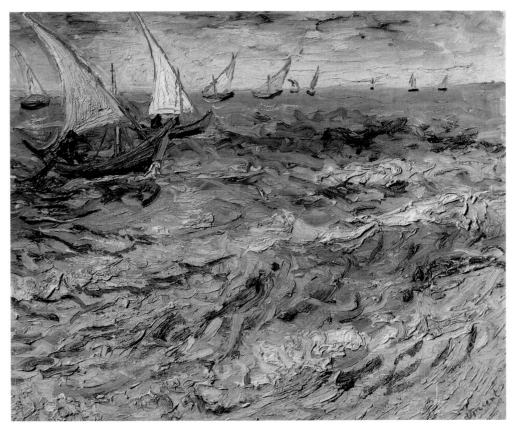

041. VINCENT VAN GOGH
Seascape at Saintes-Maries; 1888

042. VINCENT VAN GOGH
Beach with Figures and Sea with a Ship; 1882

043. LEOPOLD LE GUEN
Naval Combat between The Rights of Man *and the English Vessel*
Indefatigable *and the Frigate* Amazon; 1853

044. MAURITZ FREDERICK HENDRICK DE HAAS
Merchant Shipping off Dover; 1859

045. CHILDE HASSAM
The South Ledges, Appledore; 1913

046. CHILDE HASSAM
The Silver Veil and the Golden Gate; 1914

047. WILLIAM HODGES
A View of Cape Stephens in Cook's Straits with Waterspout; 1776

048. FERDINAND HODLER
Surprised by the Storm; 1886

049. WINSLOW HOMER
Breezing Up; 1876

050. EDWARD HOPPER
Columbia *and* Shamrock, *America's Cup*; 1899

051. EUGENE ISABEY
The Beach at Granville; 1863

052. EUGENE ISABEY
Low Tide; 1861

053. JOHN JENKINSON
A Brig Entering Liverpool; 19th Century

054. JOHAN BARTHOLD JONGKIND
Entrance to Honfleur Harbor; 1863

055. WILLIAM ADOLPHUS KNELL
A Dismantled East Indiaman in the Thames Estuary; c. 1850

056. LAURA KNIGHT
The Beach; 1908

057. FITZ HUGH LANE
Ship Star Light *in Boston Harbor; c. 1854*

058. FITZ HUGH LANE
Beached for Repairs, Duncan's Point, Gloucester; 1848

059. CLAUDE LORRAIN
Seaport at Sunset; 1639

060. CLAUDE LORRAIN
Morning in the Harbor; c. 1638

061. EDOUARD MANET
On the Beach-Suzanne and Eugene Manet at Berck; 1873

062. EDOUARD MANET
U.S.S. Kearsarge *off Boulogne-Fishing Boat Coming in before the Wind; 1864*

063. EDOUARD MANET
On the Beach at Boulogne; 1869

064. EDOUARD MANET
The Port at Calais; 1868

065. EDOUARD MANET
Toilers of the Sea; 1873

066. MAXIME MAUFRA
Red Sun; n.d

067. WILLIAM LEROY METCALF
Gloucester Harbour; 1895

068. CLAUDE MONET
Terrace at Sainte-Adresse; 1867

069. CLAUDE MONET
Regatta at Sainte-Adresse; 1867

070. CLAUDE MONET
The Cliff at Etretat; 1883

071. CLAUDE MONET
La Pointe de la Heve; 1865

072. EDWARD MORAN
The Madeleine's *Victory over the* Countess of Dufferin,
Third America's Cup Challenger, August 11, 1876; 1876

073. EDWARD MORAN
Rescue Along the Coast; 1866

074. HENRY MORET
Waiting for the Fishermen to Return; 1894

076. BERTHE MORISOT
Harbor at Nice; 1882

075. HENRY MORET
The Cliffs of Stang, Ile de Groix; 1895

077. BERTHE MORISOT
View of the Small Harbor of Lorient; 1869

078. BERTHE MORISOT
West Cowes; Isle of Wight; 1875

079. PIETER MULIER
Shipping in a Stiff Breeze in an Estuary Between Two Turkish Forts; n.d.

080. JULES NOEL
Napoleon III receiving Queen Victoria on the Bretagne *at Cherbourg, 5 August 1858*; 1859

081. WILLIAM QUILLER ORCHARRDSON
On Board HMS Bellerophon; 1880

082. CHARLES PARSONS and LYMAN ATWATER; NATHANIEL CURRIER lithographer
The New York Yacht Club Regatta; 1869

083. BONAVENTURA PEETERS
Seascape with Sailors Sheltering from a Rainstorm; c. 1640

084. JAN PEETERS
A Man-of-war Lowering Sails as a Storm Approaches; n.d.

085. CAMILLE PISSARRO
The Pilot's Jetty, Le Havre, Morning, Grey Weather, Misty; 1903

086. PIERRE-AUGUSTE RENOIR
Sea and Cliffs; c. 1884/85

088. PIERRE-AUGUSTE RENOIR
Sunset at Sea; 1879

089. JAN CLAESZ RIETSCHOOF
Dutch Ships in the Mouth of the Schelde; c. 1680s

090. ROBERT SALMON
Royal Naval Vessels off Pembroke Dock, Milford Haven; c. 1839

091. ROBERT SALMON
View of Liverpool; 1825

092. JOHN SINGER SARGENT
Oyster Gatherers at Cancale; 1878

093. CLAUDE EMILE SCHUFFENECKER
The Needle at Etretat; n.d.

094. GEORGES SEURAT
Lighthouse at Honfleur; 1886

095. GEORGES SEURAT
The Harbor at Grandcamp; 1885

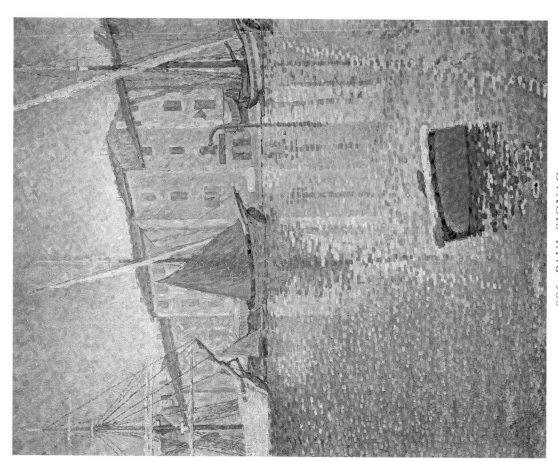

096. PAUL SIGNAC
The Red buoy, St. Tropez; 1895

098. ABRAHAM STORCK
A Fortified Mediterranean Port with an Obelisk and a Galley Moored Nearby; 1676

099. JAMES TISSOT
The Ball on Shipboard; 1874

100. J. M. W. TURNER
Van Tromp, going about to please his Masters, Ships at Sea, getting a Good Wetting; 1844

101. J. M. W. TURNER
The Fighting Temeraire *tugged to her last berth to be broken up, 1838; 1839*

102. J. M. W. TURNER
Keelmen Heaving in Coals by Moonlight; 1835

103. J. M. W. TURNER
Sun rising through vapour; fishermen cleaning and selling fish; 1807

104. JAMES GALE TYLER
*A centerboard schooner of the New York Yacht Club with a pair of steam yachts
and a small launch on Long Island Sound; n.d*

105. LOUIS VALTAT
Violet Cliffs; 1900

106. WILLEM VAN DE VELDE THE YOUNGER
An English Ship in Action with Barbary Pirates; 1680

108. WILLEM VAN DE VELDE THE YOUNGER
Two Dutch Vessels Close-Hauled in a Strong Breeze; c. 1672

109. CLAUDE-JOSEPH VERNET
*A Mediterranean Port at Sunrise with a Lighthouse, Fishermen,
and a British Two-Decker Man-of-war at Anchor; 1753*

110. CLAUDE-JOSEPH VERNET
The Shipwreck; 1772

111. CLAUDE-JOSEPH VERNET
A Mediterranean Port at Dawn; c. 1740-50

112. LIEVE VERSCHUIER
Marine; c. 1675

113. ATTRIBUTED TO SAMUEL WALTERS
The Black Ball Line clipper ship Ocean Chief *reducing sail on her Australian Run;* 1853

114. JOHN WEBBER
A Party from HMS Resolution *Shooting Sea Horses;* 1784

115. JAMES ABBOTT MCNEILL WHISTLER
Alone with the Tide; 1861

116. JAMES ABBOTT MCNEILL WHISTLER
Nocturne in Blue and Gold: Valparaiso; 1866

117. JAMES ABBOTT MCNEILL WHISTLER
Wapping; 1860-64

118. JAMES ABBOTT MCNEILL WHISTLER
The Blue Wave: Biarritz; 1862

119. ABRAHAM WILLAERTS
A Spanish Three-Decker Anchored at Naples; 1669

120. ABRAHAM WILLAERTS
A Coastal Landscape with Figures on the shore with a Spanish Man-o'-war
Putting to Sea as a Dutch Fleet Approaches; 1640

LIST OF WORKS

001. Ludolf Backhuysen (1631–1708); *A Wijdschip, a Smalschip and a States Yacht Tacking*; n.d.; oil on canvas; 25⅗" x 39" (65 x 98.8 cm)
002. Ludolf Backhuysen (1631–1708); *Dutch Vessels on a Stormy Sea*; c. 1690; oil on canvas; 26" x 31½" (66 x 80 cm)
003. George Bellows (1882–1925); *The Big Dory*; 1913; oil on canvas; 18" x 22" (45.7 x 55.8 cm)
004. Thomas Birch (1779–1851); *The* Macedonian *and the* United States; 1812; oil on canvas; 29" x 34½" (73.7 x 87.7 cm)
005. Thomas Birch (1779–1851); *The Battery and Harbor*; 1811; oil on canvas; 29" x 41" (73.7 x 104.1 cm)
006. John Blunt (1798–1835); *Boston Harbor*; 1835; oil on panel; 20 ½" x 28" (52.1 x 71.1 cm)
007. Eugene Boudin (1824–1898); *Quay at Honfleur*; 1865; oil on paper mounted on panel; 8" x 10½" (20.3 x 26.8 cm)
008. Eugene Boudin (1824–1898); *Etretat, the Porte d'Aval*; 1890; oil on canvas; 31½" x 43 ⅓" (79.9 x 109.9)
009. Eugene Boudin (1824–1898); *Quay at Villefranche*; 1892; oil on canvas; 19 ⅞" x 29 ⅜" (50.7 x 74.5 cm)
010. Eugene Boudin (1824–1898); *Beach at Trouville*; 1863; oil on panel; 13 ¾" x 22 ½" (34.9 x 57.8 cm)
011. William Bradford (1823–1892); *Ships in Boston Harbor at Twilight*; 1859; oil on prepared millboard; 11¾" x 18¾" (29.8 x 47.6 cm)
012. Jules Breton (1827–1906); *A Spring by the Sea*; 1866; oil on canvas; 43⅓" x 61" (110 x 155 cm)
013. Ford Madox Brown (1821–1893); *The Last of England*; 1855; oil on wood; 32½" x 29½" (82.5 x 75 cm)
014. James E. Buttersworth (1817–1894); *The Schooner* Mohawk *off Sandy Hook Lighthouse*; n.d.; oil on board; 9" x 12" (22.9 x 30.5 cm)
015. James E. Buttersworth (1817–1894); *Yachts Rounding the Mark*; c. 1875; oil on academy board; 7¾" x 10" (19.7 x 25.4 cm)
016. James E. Buttersworth (1817–1894); Columbia *leading* Dauntless *in the Hurricane Cup Race*; n.d.; oil on canvas; 12" x 18" (30.5 x 45.7 cm)
017. Gustave Caillebotte (1848–1894); *Regatta at Villerville*; 1884; oil on canvas; 23 ¾" x 28 ¾" (60.3 x 73 cm)
018. Jan van de Cappelle (1624–1679); *Shipping in a Calm at Flushing with a States General Yacht Firing a Salute*; 1649; oil on panel; 27⅜" x 36¼" (69.7 x 92.2 cm)
019. Jan van de Cappelle (1624–1679); *Shipping in Calm Waters of an Estuary, a Harbor Town in the Distance*; 1650; oil on panel; 16⅝" x 21⅛" (42.3 x 53.7 cm)
020. Mary Cassatt (1844–1926); *Children at the Seashore*; 1885; oil on canvas; 38 ⅔" x 29 (97.5 x 73.7)
021. Lorenzo Castro (c. 1640–1700?); *The Battle of Actium, 2 September 31 BC*; 1672; oil on canvas; 42⁷⁄₁₀" x 62⅕: (108.5 x 158 cm)
022. William Merritt Chase (1849–1916); *At the Seaside*; 1892; oil on canvas; 20" x 34" (50.8 x 86.4 cm)
023. Nicholas Matthew Condy (1816–1851); *Mr. Ward and his Family on Board his Cutter* Guerrilla; c. 1840; oil on wood panel; 13¼" x 18" (33.7 x 45.7 cm)
024. John Sell Cotman (1782–1842); *Fishing Boats off Yarmouth*; n.d.
025. Gustave Courbet (1819–1877); *The Porte d'Aval at Etretat*; 1869; oil on canvas; 31" x 50⅖" (79 x 128 cm)
026. Gustave Courbet (1819–1877); *The Fishing Boat*; 1865; oil on canvas; 25½" x 32" (64.8 x 81.3 cm)
027. Gustave Courbet (1819–1877); *The Shore at Trouville: Sunset Effect*; c. 1865/69; oil on canvas; 28" x 40⅕" (71.4 x 102.2 cm)
028. Frederic Schiller Cozzens (1846–1928) *Off Brenton's Reef*; 1883; watercolor on paper; 14" x 20¼" (35.6 x 51.4 cm)
029. Nathaniel Currier (1813–1888) and James Merritt Ives (1824–1895); *The Yacht Squadron at Newport*; 1872; lithograph in black and white with color added; 18½" x 28" (47 x 71.1 cm)
030. Aelbert Cuyp (1620–1691); *The Maas at Dordrecht*; c. 1650; oil on canvas; 45¼" x 67" (114.9 x 170.2 cm)
031. Eugene Delacroix (1798–1863); *Shipwreck on the Coast*; 1862; oil on canvas; 15¼" x 18⅜" (38.8 x 46.7 cm)
032. Thomas Eakins (1844–1916); *Starting Out after Rail*; 1874; oil on vanvas mounted on masonite; 24¼" x 19⅞" (61.6 x 50.2 cm)
033. Flemish School; *The Wreck of the* Amsterdam; c. 1610s; oil on canvas; 49⅕" x 70" (125.7 x 177.8 cm)
034. Caspar David Friedrich (1774–1840); *Moonrise at the Sea*; 1822; oil on canvas; 21⅝" x 28" (55 x 71 cm)
035. Caspar David Friedrich (1774–1840); *The Sea of Ice*; 1823-24; oil on canvas; 38⅛" x 50" (97.7 x 126.9 cm)
036. Caspar David Friedrich (1774–1840); *Periods of Life*; 1834-35; oil on canvas; 28½" x 37" (72.5 x 94 cm)
037. Thomas Gainsborough (1727–1788); *A Rocky Coastal Scene*; 1781; oil on canvas; 39½" x 50" (100.3 x 127 cm)
038. Paul Gauguin (1848–1903); *Bathers at Dieppe*; 1885, oil on canvas; 15" x 18⅛" (38.1 x 46 cm)
039. Paul Gauguin (1848–1903); *Seascape*; 1886; oil on canvas; 28" x 36¼" (71.1 x 92.1 cm)
040. Vincent Van Gogh (1853–1890); *Boats on the Beach at Saintes-Maries*; 1888; oil on canvas; 25½" x 31¾" (64.5 x 81 cm)
041. Vincent Van Gogh (1853–1890); *Seascape at Saintes-Maries*; 1888; oil on canvas; 17⅜" x 20⅞" (44 x 53 cm)
042. Vincent Van Gogh (1853–1890); *Beach with Figures and Sea with a Ship*; 1882; oil on paper on cardboard; 13⅗" x 20" (34.5 x 51 cm)
043. Leopold Le Guen (1828–1895); *Naval Combat between* The Rights of Man *and the English Vessel* Indefatigable *and the Frigate* Amazon; 1853; oil on canvas; 38⅜" x 51⅜" (97.5 x 130.5 cm)
044. Mauritz Frederick Hendrick de Haas; (1832–1895); *Merchant Shipping off Dover*; 1859; oil on canvas; 33½" x 45½" (85.1 x 115.6 cm)
045. Childe Hassam (1859–1935); *The South Ledges, Appledore*; 1913; oil on canvas; 42⅛" x 54¼" (107 x 137.8 cm)
046. Childe Hassam (1859–1935); *The Silver Veil and the Golden Gate*; 1914; oil on canvas; 30" x 32" (76.2 x 81.3 cm(
047. William Hodges (1744–1797); *A View of Cape Stephens in Cook's Straits with Waterspout*; 1776; oil on canvas; 53½" x 76" (135.9 x 193 cm)
048. Ferdinand Hodler (1853–1918); *Surprised by the Storm*; 1886; oil on canvas; 39⅖" x 51⅕" (100 x 130 cm)
049. Winslow Homer (1836–1910); *Breezing Up*; 1876; oil on canvas; 24⅛" x 38⅛" (61.5 x 97 cm)
050. Edward Hopper (1882–1967); Columbia *and* Shamrock, *America's Cup*; 1899; watercolor on paper; 9" x 10¾" (23 x 27.3)
051. Eugene Isabey (1803–1886); *The Beach at Granville*; 1863; oil on canvas; 32⁷⁄₁₀" x 48⅘" (83 x 124 cm)
052. Eugene Isabey (1803–1886); *Low Tide*; 1861; oil on canvas; 33" x 48⅘" (84 x 124 cm)
053. John Jenkinson (c. 1790–1823); *A Brig Entering Liverpool*; 19th Century; oil on canvas; 19" x 27½" (48.5 x 69.8 cm)
054. Johan Barthold Jongkind (1819–1891); *Entrance to Honfleur Harbor*; 1863; oil on canvas; 13⅛" x 18¼" (33.3 x 46.3 cm)
055. William Adolphus Knell (1802–1875); *A Dismantled East Indiaman in the Thames Estuary*; c. 1850; oil on canvas; 48"x 60" (122.2 x 152.5 cm)
056. Laura Knight (1877–1970); *The Beach*; 1908; oil on canvas; 50¼" x 60 ¼" (127.5 x 153 cm)
057. Fitz Hugh Lane (1804–1865); *Ship* Star Light *in Boston Harbor*; c. 1854; oil on canvas; 23¾" x 25½" (60.3 x 64.8 cm)
058. Fitz Hugh Lane (1804–1865); *Beached for Repairs, Duncan's Point, Gloucester*; 1848; oil on canvas; 16¼" x 22⅛" (41.3 x 56.2)
059. Claude Lorrain (c. 1600–1682); *Seaport at Sunset*; 1639; oil on canvas; 40½" x 54" (103 x 137 cm)
060. Claude Lorrain (c. 1600–1682); *Morning in the Harbor*; c. 1638; oil on canvas; 29⅛" x 38³⁄₁₆" (74 x 97 cm)
061. Edouard Manet (1832–1883); *On the Beach-Suzanne and Eugene Manet at Berck*; 1873; oil on canvas; 23½" x 28⅞" (59.6 x 73.2)
062. Edouard Manet (1832–1883); *U.S.S.* Kearsarge *off Boulogn*, *Fishing Boat Coming in before the Wind*; 1864; oil on canvas; 32⅛" x 39⅜" (81.6 x 100cm)

063. Edouard Manet (1832–1883); *On the Beach at Boulogne*; 1869; oil on canvas; 12¾" x 26" (32.4 x 66 cm)
064. Edouard Manet (1832–1883); *The Port at Calais*; 1868; oil on canvas; 32⅛" x 39⅝" (81.5 x 100.7 cm)
065. Edouard Manet (1832–1883); *Toilers of the Sea*; 1873, oil on canvas; 24¾" x 31¼" (63 x 79.3 cm)
066. Maxime Maufra (1861–1918); *Red Sun*; n.d.; oil on canvas; 17⅝" x 23⅝" (44.9 x 60.1 cm)
067. William Leroy Metcalf (1858–1925); *Gloucester Harbour*; 1895; oil on canvas; 26" x 28⅔" (66 x 73 cm)
068. Claude Monet (1840–1926); *Terrace at Sainte-Adresse*; 1867; oil on canvas; 38⅝" x 51⅛" (98.1 x 129.9 cm)
069. Claude Monet (1840–1926); *Regatta at Sainte-Adresse*; 1867; oil on canvas; 29⅗" x 40" (75.2 x 101.6 cm)
070. Claude Monet (1840–1926); *The Cliff at Etretat*; 1883; oil on canvas; 23⅘" x 32⅕" (60.5 x 81.8 cm)
071. Claude Monet (1840–1926); *La Pointe de la Heve*; 1865; oil on canvas; 35½" x 59" (90 x 150 cm)
072. Edward Moran (1829–1901); *The* Madeleine's *Victory over the* Countess of Dufferin, *Third Americas's Cup Challenger, August 11, 1876*; 1876; oil on canvas; 23" x 37" (58.4 x 94 cm)
073. Edward Moran (1829–1901); *Rescue Along the Coast*; 1866; oil on canvas; 42" x 66" (106.8 x 167.7 cm)
074. Henry Moret (1856–1913); *Waiting for the Fishermen to Return*; 1894; oil on canvas; 21⅜" x 25⅝" (54.5 x 65.3cm)
075. Henry Moret (1856–1913); *The Cliffs of Stang, Ile de Groix*; 1895; oil on canvas; 36¼" x 28⅝" (92.1 x 73 cm)
076. Berthe Morisot (1841–1895); *Harbor at Nice*; 1882; oil on paper mounted on canvas; 23¼" x17 (59 x 43 cm)
077. Berthe Morisot (1841–1895); *View of the Small Harbor of Lorient*; 1869; oil on canvas; 16⅞" x 28⅜" (55.2 x 72.2 cm)
078. Berthe Morisot (1841–1895); *West Cowes; Isle of Wight*; 1875; oil on canvas; 18⅞" x 14⅛" (48 x 36 cm)
079. Pieter Mulier (1637–1701); *Shipping in a Stiff Breeze in an Estuary Between Two Turkish Forts*; n.d.; oil on canvas; 19⅞" x 26¾" (50.5 x 68 cm)
080. Jules Noel (1810–1891); *Napoleon III receiving Queen Victoria on the* Bretagne *at Cherbourg, 5 August 1858*; 1859, oil on canvas; 64⅘" x 90" (164.5 x 228.5 cm)
081. William Quiller Orcharrdson (1832–1910); *On Board HMS* Bellerophon; 1880; oil on canvas; 65" x 98" (164.9 x 248.6 cm)
082. Charles Parsons (1821–1910) and Lyman Atwater (19th cent.); Nathaniel Currier (1813–1888) lithographer; *The New York Yacht Club Regatta*; 1869; lithograph with color added; 20¼" x 28¾" (51.4 x 73 cm)
083. Bonaventura Peeters (1614–1652); *Seascape with Sailors Sheltering from a Rainstorm*; c. 1640; oil on panel; 13" x 18" (33 x 45.7 cm)
084. Jan Peeters (1624–1680); *A Man-of-war Lowering Sails as a Storm Approaches*; n.d.; oil on panel; 32" x 44" (81.5 x 111.5 cm)
085. Camille Pissarro (1830–1903); *The Pilot's Jetty, Le Havre, Morning, Grey Weather, Misty*; 1903; oil on canvas; 25⅗" x 32" (65 x 81.3 cm)
086. Pierre-Auguste Renoir (1841–1919); *Sea and Cliffs*; c. 1884/85; oil on canvas; 20⅕" x 25" (51.4 x 63.5 cm)
087. Pierre-Auguste Renoir (1841–1919); *By the Seashore*; 1883; oil on canvas; 36⅓" x 28½" (92.1 x 72.4 cm)
088. Pierre-Auguste Renoir (1841–1919); *Sunset at Sea*; 1879; oil on canvas; 18" x 24" (45.7 x 61 cm)
089. Jan Claesz Rietschoof (1652–1719); *Dutch Ships in the Mouth of the Schelde*; c. 1680s; oil on panel; 13½" x 18" (34.3 x 45.8 cm)
090. Robert Salmon (1775–after 1845); *Royal Naval Vessels off Pem-*
roke Dock, Milford Haven; c. 1839; oil on canvas; 26¼" x 40¾" (66.7
5 cm)
rt Salmon (1775–after 1845); *View of Liverpool*; 1825; oil on
15 ¾" x 25" (40 x 63.5 cm)
Sargent (1856–1925); *Oyster Gatherers at Cancale*;
31" x 50½" (79 x 128.3 cm)
e Schuffenecker (1851–1934) *The Needle at Etretat*;
n.d.; oil on canvas; 12⅝" x 16⅛" (32.4 x 41 cm)
094. Georges Seurat (1859–1891); *Lighthouse at Honfleur*; 1886, oil on canvas; 26¼" x 32¼" (66.7 x 81.9 cm)
095. Georges Seurat (1859–1891); *The Harbor at Grandcamp*; 1885; oil on canvas; 25⅝" x 32" (65 x 81.2 cm)
096. Paul Signac (1863–1935); *The Red buoy, St. Tropez*; 1895; oil on canvas; 31⅞" x 25½" (81 x 65 cm)
097. Clarkson Stanfield (1793–1867); *On the Dogger Bank*; 1846; oil on canvas; 30" x 27½" (76.1 x 69.8 cm)
098. Abraham Storck (1644–1708); *A Fortified Mediterranean Port with an Obelisk and a Galley Moored Nearby*; 1676; oil on panel; 18½" x 24⅜" (47 x 63 cm)
099. James Tissot (1836–1902); *The Ball on Shipboard*; 1874; oil on canvas; 33" x 51" (84.1 x 129.5 cm)
100. J. M. W. Turner (1775–1851); *Van Tromp, going about to please his Masters, Ships at Sea, getting a Good Wetting*; 1844; oil on canvas; 36" x 48" (91.4 x 121.9 cm)
101. J. M. W. Turner (1775–1851); *The Fighting* Temeraire *tugged to her last berth to be broken up, 1838*; 1839; oil on canvas; 35¾" x 48" (90.8 x 122 cm)
102. J. M. W. Turner (1775–1851); *Keelmen Heaving in Coals by Moonlight*; 1835; oil on canvas; 36⅜" x 48⅜" (92.3 x 122.8 cm)
103. J. M. W. Turner (1775–1851); *Sun rising through vapour; fishermen cleaning and selling fish*; 1807; oil on canvas; 53" x 70½" (134.6 x 179.1 cm)
104. James Gale Tyler (1855–1931); *A centerboard schooner of the New York Yacht Club with a pair of steam yachts and a small launch on Long Island Sound*; n.d.; oil on canvas; 31" x 44" (78.7 x 111.8 cm)
105. Louis Valtat (1869–1952); *Violet Cliffs*; 1900, oil on canvas; 25 13/16" x 32 ⅛" (65.5 x 81.5 cm)
106. Willem van de Velde the Younger (1633–1707); *An English Ship in Action with Barbary Pirates*; 1680; oil on canvas; 40⅜" x 57" (102.7 x 147 cm)
107. Willem van de Velde the Younger (1633–1707); *An English Royal Yacht and Others Shipping in Heavy Seas*; c. 1675; oil on canvas; 51" x 42" (129.5 x 106.5 cm)
108. Willem van de Velde the Younger (1633–1707); *Two Dutch Vessels Close-Hauled in a Strong Breeze*; c. 1672; oil on canvas; 17¼" x 21⅞" (43.8 x 55.7 cm)
109. Claude-Joseph Vernet (1714–1789); *A Mediterranean Port at Sunrise with a Lighthouse, Fishermen, and a British Two-Decker Man-of-war at Anchor*; 1753; oil on canvas; 19⅛" x 31¾" (48.6 x 80.5 cm)
110. Claude-Joseph Vernet (1714–1789); *The Shipwreck*; 1772; oil on canvas; 44⅝" x 64⅛" (113.5 x 162.9 cm)
111. Claude-Joseph Vernet (1714–1789); *A Mediterranean Port at Dawn*; c. 1740-50; oil on canvas; 28⅝" x 53" (72.7 x 134.9 cm)
112. Lieve Verschuier (1630–1686); *Marine*; c. 1675; oil on canvas; 35 ⅛" x 44 11/16" (89.2 x 113.5 cm)
113. Attributed to Samuel Walters (1811–1882); *The Black Ball Line clipper ship* Ocean Chief *reducing sail on her Australian Run*; 1853; oil on canvas; 26" x 40" (66 x 101.6 cm)
114.John Webber (1751–1793); *A Party from HMS* Resolution *Shooting Sea Horses*; 1784; oil on canvas; 49" x 62" (124.5 x 157.5 cm)
115. James Abbott McNeill Whistler (1834–1903); *Alone with the Tide*; 1861; oil on canvas; 34⅓" x 46" (87.2 x 116.7 cm)
116. James Abbott McNeill Whistler (1834–1903); *Nocturne in Blue and Gold: Valparaiso*; 1866; oil on canvas; 29¾" x 39" (75.6 x 99 cm)
117. James Abbott McNeill Whistler (1834–1903); *Wapping*; 1860-64; oil on canvas; 28⅜" x 40⅛" (71.1 x 101.6 cm)
118. James Abbott McNeill Whistler (1834–1903); *The Blue Wave: Biarritz*; 1862; oil on canvas; 24½" x 34½" (62.2 x 87.6 cm)
119. Abraham Willaerts (1603–1669); *A Spanish Three-Decker Anchored at Naples*; 1669; oil on canvas; 34" x 21½" (86.4 x 54.6 cm)
120. Abraham Willaerts (1603–1669); *A Coastal Landscape with Figures on the shore with a Spanish Man-o'-war Putting to Sea as a Dutch Fleet Approaches*; 1640; oil on oak panel; 30½" x 42" (77.5 x 107 cm)